ISIS: The Church's Wake-Up Call!

Aaron B. Claxton, PHD

ISIS: The Church's Wake-Up Call!

Copyright © 2015 by Aaron B. Claxton, PHD

All rights reserved. No part of this book may be reproduced, stored in retrieval system, or transmitted in any form or by any means – electronic, mechanical, photocopy, recording, or otherwise – except for brief quotations in printed reviews, without written permission of the author.

Unless otherwise noted, Scripture is taken from The Holy Bible, The King James Version (KJV). The King James Version is in the public domain.

ISBN 9780996404013

Library of Congress Control Number: 2015949736

> Published by Kingdom Kaught Publishing, LLC
> Odenton, MD 21113

> First Printing 2015
> Printed in the USA

DEDICATION

It gives me great pleasure to dedicate this book to my beloved and indispensable wife, of nearly 58 years. She is not only my lover, and confidante, but also my helper, critic and encourager in everything I do- including this book.

She is forever my proofreader, advisor and all that I have ever needed in this business of book writing.

Dr. Deborah J. Claxton has earned several degrees and has of late received her doctorate of Religious Education-and is an author in her own right.

Thank God for "Dr. Deborah," as she is affectionately known by many, and "Sugar Lump," as she is known by me.

Table of Contents

Chapter 1 - *The Beginning of Islam* 1

Chapter 2 - *Christ Chosen to Rule from Eternity* 5

Chapter 3 - *The Rise of Isis, A Sign* 9

Chapter 4 - *Islam Speaks False Prophecy* 13

Chapter 5 - *Quranic verses Quoted* 17

Chapter 6 - *Martyrdom - A Fact of Early Church History and an Endtime Church Reality* 21

Chapter 7 - *Why Persecution and Martyrdom?* 33

Chapter 8 - *A Deeper Look into Islam's False Prophecies* 39

Chapter 9 - *Understanding God's Timeline as We Approach the End* 43

Chapter 10 - *ISIS, The Church's Wake-Up Call!* 51

Chapter 11 - *The Time Has Arrived for a Revived Muslim Caliphate* 57

Final Chapter 61

Bibliography 67

The Beginning of Islam

The church is ordained of God to be His beacon light to the world, even as Israel was that light in Old Testament times. ISIS means: "The Islamic State of Iraq and Syria."

ISIS declared itself the "Islamic State" in June of 2014. They began to promote their notoriety by viciously attacking ancient Christian settlements in the vicinity of the ancient Bible City known as Nineveh. Some of these Christian settlements date back to the 1st Century A.D.

Their fear tactics were and are to behead men publicly, and to rape and enslave Christian women and children. Nineveh is located not far from the modern city known as Mosul which ISIS also overthrew and occupies.

ISIS: The Church's Wake-Up Call!

ISIS terrorists hate the Bible, Christians and Jews so fiercely, that they found, desecrated and destroyed the tomb of the Old Testament prophet Jonah! Of course this is an old practice of Islam.

ISIS afterwards attacked ancient Christian enclaves in Syria, where they repeated and increased their atrocities on Christians, by crucifying them, as well as beheading others. Their purpose is to strike fear in Westerners and middle Easterners who have not yet submitted to their terrorism!

Islam became the church's and the Jew's arch enemy from its inception; even as Satan became God's archenemy after his rebellion and casting out of heaven.

ISIS is of the devil, just as the church is of God. ISIS is on the outermost, radical fringe of Islam, trying to assert their "right" to world domination which Islam walked in for 1400 years!

They lost their supremacy in 1924, when "Christian," Western powers defeated the Ottoman Empire in Turkey. This Islamic empire was replete with its Caliphate, i.e., its Pope-like global ruler. The Caliphate has been located in such countries as Iraq, Egypt, Sudan and Turkey--the last location. Each Caliph is supposed to be a descendant of Muhammed, and a Shiite.

When Muhammed, a descendant of Ishmael, had a spirit appear to him calling Allah "the only god and Muhammed his prophet", Islam was birthed by Satan, in 610 A.D! Islam means submission, not peace. Muhammed was deceived by that spirit that, they, the Muslims, are

God's chosen people; that they were/are God's chosen world rulers. That was a lie! Their method of controlling others is by murder, fear, and lying! These are the characteristics of the devil (St. John 8:44-45; St. John 4:18).

Islam burst onto the world scene 2600 years after Abraham founded Judaism! Muhammed declared in 610 A.D. that "There is no god but Allah, and Muhammed is his messenger." He went forth to build his army of soldiers by robbing camel trains and by spreading his new religion with the sword. All those who submitted to Allah became a part of Muhammed's religion. Men who refused were killed, whereas women were raped or made unwilling wives or sex slaves. ISIS is continuing this practice today. These evil actions are not new! They began with Muhammed himself some 1400 years ago!

Muhammed forced a false "god" on the world after the true God, Yahweh Elohim, through the centuries had proven to the world that He is the One and Only, True and Living God, by His many miraculous acts recorded in the Bible. The ten prophesied plagues on Egypt that were fulfilled; the openings of the Red Sea and the River Jordan; the supernatural victories He gave Israel over her enemies (even in modern times); and especially the raising of Jesus Christ from the dead! And finally Yahweh's defeats of Israel's modern day enemies!

Christ Chosen to Rule from Eternity

On the other hand, Jehovah God, spoke in His eternal counsel saying, "Yet I have set my king (Jesus the Messiah) upon my holy hill of Zion" (That is Jerusalem).

Jehovah proceeded to decree, "You are my Son; this day have I begotten you. Ask of me, and I shall give you the nations for your inheritance and the uttermost (farthest flung) parts of the earth for your possession. You shall break them (heathen nations, i.e., Islam) with a rod of iron; you shall dash them in pieces like a potter's vessel." (Psalm 2:2-9)

ISIS: The Church's Wake-Up Call!

Short version: God gave the rulership and ownership of the world and its inhabitants and land to His Son, Jesus the Messiah, to rule and own forever (Hebrews 1:1-4)! Whenever ISIS seeks to rule the world by the old satanic methods of murder, fear and lying, God or Messiah's rule is by giving eternal life, love and truth to every person who will believe!

Psalm 72 speaks of "the Glory and Universality of Messiah's Reign." That Psalm says: "Give to the king Your judgements, O God…He shall have dominion also from sea to sea, and from the River to the ends of the earth."

"Those who dwell in the wilderness will bow before Him, and His enemies will lick the dust (like the serpent). The kings of Tarshish and of the isles (gentiles) will bring presents:

"The kings of Sheba and Seba (Arabs) will offer gifts. Yes, all kings shall fall down before Him; "All nations shall serve Him." (Psalm 72:1, 8-11)(Emphasis mine)

Psalm 110 says: "The LORD shall send the rod of your strength out of Zion, Rule in the midst of your enemies… The LORD is at your right hand; He shall execute kings in the day of His wrath. He shall judge among the nations…He shall execute the heads of many countries" (Psalm 110:2, 5-6b). Beloveds, the Bible speaks here of Jesus the Messiah, in the end, ruling in all His splendor, glory and might (See Luke 21:27).

The Rise of Isis, A Sign

The "sleeping giant" called Islam is currently stirring itself up in the group called ISIS, and displaying the old Islamic practices of beheading, raping, enslaving and taking the property of others. (This is Satan's way!) ISIS' rising up is a sign from God that the end is at hand!

Isaiah Chapter 14 characterizes Lucifer as the "king of Babylon" (a Muslim nation today) who was cast down from heaven. We find this casting down recorded here is also found in Luke 10:19 and Revelation 12:12-13. Isaiah 14:12 says, "How are you fallen from heaven, O Lucifer, son of the morning (same name as Allah)? How are you cut down to the ground who weakened the nations! For you have said in your heart, 'I will ascend into heaven; I will exalt my throne above the stars of God. I will sit upon the mount of the congregation, in the sides of the north, I will ascend above the heights of the clouds; I will be like the most high.'" (These are the five evil insults to God, because of evil pride!)

"Yet you will be brought down to hell to the sides of the pit. They that see you shall narrowly look upon you, and consider you, saying, 'is this the man that made the earth to tremble, that shook kingdoms; that made the world, as a wilderness, and destroyed the cities thereof; that opened not the house of his prisoners" (Isaiah 14:12-17). The world is shaking now because of ISIS! The man, "king of Babylon," is none other than the Muslim Antichrist!

Let us also consult Daniel 7:23-25, and Revelation 13:4-10.

In Daniel 7:23:25, Daniel writes the angelic explanation of this particular night vision: "He gave me this explanation: The fourth beast is a fourth kingdom that will appear on earth. It will be different from all the other (preceding) kingdoms (a religious, military, political kingdom) and will devour the whole earth, trampling it down and crushing it…He will speak against the Most High and oppress (persecute) his saints and try to change set times and the laws."

Revelation 13:5-6 says: "The beast was given a mouth to utter proud words and blasphemies (against the Most High) and exercise his (the devil's) authority for forty-months. He opened his mouth to blaspheme God, and to slander his name…He was given power to make war against the saints and to conquer them."

The fourth beast cannot be Rome. Rome didn't do the atrocious things cited above. Rome didn't destroy lands; they simply annexed conquered lands and made them a part of the Roman Empire. Islam crushed and destroyed people and lands!

For all of the above matters to make sense, one must consider that the Bible contains true prophecy; whereas, the Hadith (a book of Muhammed's sacred sayings) contains false prophecy. Philosophically speaking, there can only be one of any given thing of a specific category, and time. There can only be one true God at a time! The prophet Isaiah recorded Yahweh's own words that say, "I am the Lord, and there is no one else, there is no God besides me" (Isaiah 45:5). The psalmist wrote and said (get the true picture), "For Yahweh is great and greatly to be praised: he is to be feared above all gods. For the gods of the nations are idols: but Yahweh made the heavens" (Psalm 96:4-5).

Here the Holy Bible declares that among all other "gods" Yahweh alone is the True God, and Creator of the heavens (as well as the earth), and that all other "gods" are idols! Idols that were made by men's hands and imaginations! Isaiah, God's prophet of old, wrote his prophecies some 1400 years before Islam was concocted! Islam borrowed heavily from the Old and New Testaments, and grossly distorted their teachings! They accuse the Jews and Christians of "corrupting" the Bible. No, they are the ones who did that!

Islam Speaks False Prophecy

Islamic "prophecies" teach that in the end time (now) they will be restored to world rulership, with the arising of their Caliph, and the re-establishing of a world-ruling Caliphate! That is what ISIS is purporting to be and have right now with Al Bagdadi in Iraq. However, some of their other denominations such as the Shiites, in Iran have another view. Their view is of the rising of a chief leader-called the Mahdi (The Muslim Messiah), after several centuries. Islam wants to create as much havoc and confusion in the world as possible to bring forth the Mahdi, the Muslim "Messiah"! They also falsely teach that Jesus (ISA) is a Muslim; and that when he returns he will force all Christians to become Muslims! What a lie from a religion built on lies! This is the most antichristian religion on earth! Islam believes that the Mahdi or the Antichrist will restore world order and peace.

They get this idea from the Judeo-Christian Bible! Daniel 9:26-27 speaks of "the ruler who will come…He will confirm a "peace" covenant with many for one' seven' (one week of seven years). In the middle of the 'seven' he will put an end to sacrifice and offerings …" (He, the Antichrist will break the peace covenant with the Jews after 3 ½ years).

Islam's false creed, the Shahadatan, is both false and blasphemous! It is the most anti-Yahweh, anti-Christ religious declaration on earth! This creed denies the holy Trinity, Jesus Christ's Divine Incarnation as the Son of God--as well as Christ's death, burial and resurrection!

The two elements of this creed, the Shahadatan, are:

1. Allah is the only one true supreme God and,
2. Muhammed (The Praised One) is the seal and final messenger of Allah. What a LIE!

Islam Speaks False Prophecy

At least one Eastern-thinking biblical scholar and Christian prophecy teacher, Walid Shoebat, believes that the Apostle John in Revelation 13:16-18 possibly saw Arabic symbols, instead of Greek words (pages 368-372 in Shoebat's voluminous book records these thoughts and possibilities). The book: "God's War on Terror, Islam, Prophecy and the Bible," is Shoebat's great work.

Walid Shoebat, a former Muslim terrorist turned Christian, observed something quite similar between Revelation 13:16-17 and his former faith, Islam, that the wearing of badges on Muslims' foreheads and arms inscribed with a blasphemous slogan (The Shahadatan) to distinguish them from non-Muslims, is a part of Islamic practices.

Shoebat observed that the above-mentioned practices were enjoined on Muslims in the Qur'an, Sura 27:82, and would happen in the end days with regard to the "beast of the earth" (Rev. 13:11) (p.369).

How is it that Islam comes up with the same language and imagery as the Bible, which was canonized 500 years before Islam was concocted? Simple! They borrowed from the Bible (the Book of Revelation) and slipped ideas from the Bible into their false prophecies!

Quranic verses Quoted

Beheadings and other forms of killings are taught in the Quran (Surah 8:12; Surah 47:4; Surah 9:14; Surah 9:10)

Surah 8:12-14 says "I will put terror in the hearts of non-Muslims. So cut off their necks and cut off every fingertip. Do that because they opposed Allah and His Apostle…"

Surah 47:4 says, "And when you meet those who misbelieved, in Jihad, cut off their heads until you have massacred them, and taken them captive."

Surah 8:39 says: "And keep fighting them until there is no division among you, and Islam is the only religion…"

Surah 9:29 says: "Fight those who don't believe in Allah or in the Last Day…; and don't have Islam, the religion of truth, as their religion; from among the Jews and Christians until they pay the fine for being non-Muslims and they have been humiliated."

These quotes from the Qur'an, are from the booklet, "Islam, Religion of Peace or War?" (2014, pp.24-28, The Truth)

Before we go further, let us cite a New Testament witness of the True and Living God.

The Apostle John wrote the following: "And we know that the Son of God is come, and hath given us an understanding, that we may know him that is true, and we are in him that is true even in his Son Jesus Christ. This is the true God, and eternal life."
"Little children keep yourselves from idols (false gods). Amen." (I John 5:20-21)

Thus we have the New Testament, biblical, description of the True and Living God!

Quranic verses Quoted

The book of Revelation captures the works of the devil throughout history right down to the present time. The Word says: "Woe to the inhabitants of the earth and of the sea! For the devil is come unto you, having great wrath, because he knoweth that he hath but a short time. And when the dragon saw that he was cast unto the earth, he (through his agents) persecuted the woman (Israel) which brought forth the man child (the Messiah)… and the dragon was wroth with the woman (Israel), and went to make war with the remnant of her seed (Christians) which keep the commandments of God and have the testimony of Jesus Christ" (Rev. 12:12-13, 17). Muslims have attacked Jews and Christians unprovoked, since their 7th century A.D. inception. This is a fact of history!

By the way, let me make this observation now! There are biblical prophetic markers that point, in the Bible, to the Antichrist being a Muslim! First of all, let me point out that Islam has been the chief Anti-Christian and Anti-Jewish religion for the past 1500 years! Even Hitler admired their vicious, killing ways!

Isaiah the prophet points out "The king of Babylon," and asks, "Is this the man that made the earth to tremble, that did shake the kingdoms; that made the world a wilderness…?" (Isaiah 14:4, 16-17). Daniel the prophet pointed out the little horn out of the fourth beast (empire) trampled and crushed all the three empires before it. This is the Antichrist of Islam, the fourth beast.

The prophet Micah, an 8th century prophet, (along with Isaiah who prophesied of the birth of Jesus the Messiah) also foretells the deliverance of Israel from the hand of "the Assyrian," another name for the Muslim Antichrist!

Martyrdom - A Fact of Early Church History and an Endtime Church Reality

A verse of one of the church's well known hymns says: "As it was the beginning, it now and ever shall be, World without end, Amen and Amen."

The early Christian church experienced martyrdom for some three hundred years of its existence. That is until Constantine, the first "Christian" Roman emperor, outlawed persecution against the Church. Emperor Constantine's edict to end the persecution of Christians went forth around 300 A.D., when Christianity was made the official religion of Rome.

However, in 610 AD, a new, fierce, trampling down, persecuting religion was birthed, called "Mohammedism," after its founder, Mohammed. He and his band (later an army of 10,000 soldiers) went forth killing and persecuting Christians, Jews and anyone who would not submit to his religion. Islam means submission!

As Jesus, in His bloodied state, was trudging up Golgotha's hill with His cross (along with Simon of Cyrene), Luke wrote: "A large number of people followed him, including women who mourned and wailed for him. Jesus turned and said, 'Daughters of Jerusalem, do not weep for me; weep for yourselves and for your children…For if men do these things when the tree is green, what will happen when it is dry?' "(Luke 23:28-31) (NIV)

Jesus seems to be saying, "If men treat me so viciously, and I am the beginning of Christianity (the church) what do you suppose will happen to Christians in the end times?"

I was reminded in a recent Christian International City Tour Conference in Alexandria, Virginia, that the church of Jesus Christ is the only entity on earth through which mankind can be saved and reconciled to

God. Bishop Bill Hamon, founder and covering Bishop, of Christian International Ministries, was the keynote speaker. He reminded us of his first book The Eternal Church wherein he sets forth the church of the Lord Jesus Christ as God's unique, great agency for bringing mankind to Christ. He set forth in this message the fact that three things must happen before Christ can return in His Second Coming.

They are as follows:
1. The cup of iniquity of the wickedness of man must be filled up (See Genesis 15:26 and Revelation 14:10);
2. The church must reach full maturity or be perfected, and;
3. The Kingdom of God must be established in the earth. By the way, Bishop Bill Hamon is my own beloved spiritual covering in the Christian International Apostolic Network, and has been so for many years!

I read Bishop's book on The Eternal Church in the 1980's, and the Holy Spirit dealt with my heart recently on one of the three things Bishop said was necessary to happen before Christ returns. That is the perfecting of the Church. Although the exalted Lord gave the church the five-fold ministry gifts for our perfecting, my eyes were illuminated to see and remember that the Captain of our salvation, the Lord Jesus Christ, "though He was a Son, yet He learned obedience by the things which He suffered. And having been perfected, He became the author of eternal salvation to all who obey Him" (Hebrews 5:8-9).

Here we see Jesus being perfected through suffering! Then, what about His awesome Body, the Church? The five-fold ministry gifts, do train and equip us in the things of God, but the Bible indicates strongly that the church's way into perfection and glory will be by way of tribulation and testing. The Apostle Paul strengthened the saints at Lystra, Iconium and Antioch after he had been stoned and left for dead outside of Derbe, saying, "We must through many tribulations enter the Kingdom of God" (Acts 14:22). Again, Daniel wrote concerning the end time Church: "many shall be purified, made white and refined" (Daniel 12:10). Could this be a part of the perfecting process of the end time Church? I think so!

The Apostle Peter (also Paul and John) associates Christian suffering with our glorification and perfection, which is to come. Peter wrote the following: "Beloved, do not think it strange concerning the fiery trial (beheadings by ISIS, etc.) which is to try you, as though some strange thing happened to you; but rejoice to the extent that you partake of Christ's sufferings, that when His glory is revealed, you may also be glad with exceeding joy" (I Peter 2:12-13).

As we explore this truth further, we come to see that Christian sufferings are sometimes perpetrated by God himself, in the perfecting process of His Church. Peter goes on to say, "If anyone suffers as a Christian, let him not be ashamed, but let him glorify God in this matter. For the time has come for judgement to begin at the house of God, and if it begins with us first, what will be the end of those who do not obey the gospel of God?...Therefore let those who suffer according to the will of God commit their souls to Him in doing good, as a faithful Creator" (I Peter 2:17, 19).

Please let us be informed that the above mentioned judgement at the house of God is not due to God's displeasure because of sin, but rather, these persecutions and afflictions are for the Christians' advancement and refining--a part of our perfecting and preparation for our glorification! (See 2 Thess. 1:4-5)

The Amplified Bible's rendering of Hebrews 5:8-9 reads as follows:

"Although He (Jesus) was a Son, He learned (active, special) obedience through what He suffered and, (His completed experience) making Him perfectly equipped). He became the Author and source of eternal salvation to all those who give heed and obey Him."

In the book of Revelation, Chapter 2, Jesus Christ, The Risen and glorified Lord, spoke to the church at Smyrna with these words: "Do not be afraid of what you are about to suffer. I tell you, the devil will put some of you in prison to test you, and you will suffer persecution for ten days. Be faithful, even to the point of death, and I will give you the crown of life" (Revelation 2:10).

To the church in Philadelphia, the Risen Lord said, "I am coming soon. Hold on to what you have, so that no one will take your crown. He who overcomes I will make a pillar in the temple of my God" (Revelation 3:11-12).

We read again the Revelation 12:9-12, "The great dragon was hurled down--that ancient serpent called, the devil, or Satan…He was hurled to the earth, and his angels with him…For the accuser of our brothers, who accuses them before God day and night, has been hurled down.

"They overcame him by the blood of the Lamb and by the word of their testimony; they did not love their lives so much as to shrink from death." (NIV)

Are you beginning to get the picture of what God has shown us in His Word of the reality of persecution and martyrdom slated for Christ's Church in "the end of days"? This has already begun in Iraq, Syria, Egypt, Libya, Sudan and other places around the world!

Beloveds, this is not a fairytale, as our Pretribulationist brethren try to tell us. Some teach so glibly on television and in books etc., that the church will "escape all of this in the Rapture and go to heaven for seven years." Hogwash!

Do you really want to know what the Bible says about this? Revelation 12:17 says "Then the dragon was enraged with the woman (Israel, symbolically speaking) and went off to make war against the rest of her offspring--those who obey God's commandments (I John 3:23-24) and hold to the testimony of Jesus." Beloved, the latter are Christian believers. Make no mistake about it!

Let us observe the words of Jesus in Revelation 16:15: "Behold, I come like a thief! Blessed is he who stays awake (the church must awaken from man-made fables) and keep his clothes with him, so that he may not go naked and be shamefully exposed." (NIV Version)

The Pretribulationists teach that Jesus came and raptured the church to heaven in Revelation 4:1. Apparently Jesus does not believe that! Because we see by Christ's own warning that He had not come in Revelation 16:15! And the Risen Christ is apparently warning Christians in that verse. The Pretribulationists' books and movies on "Left Behind,"etc. are unbiblical and man-made fables!

By the way, the Greek word martyr means a witness! In Revelation 17:5-6, John wrote about "MYSTERY BABYLON THE GREAT THE MOTHER OF PROSTITUTES AND OF THE ABOMINATIONS OF THE EARTH! I saw that the woman (Mystery Babylon) (Mecca, Arabia where Islam was born and, Iraq, where false religion was birthed) (Genesis 11:1-4), was drunk with the blood of the saints, (Christians) the blood of those who bore witness to Jesus."

I believe it would be good here to compare the rendering of St. Luke 21:36 in both the New King James Version of the Bible and Today's English Version of the New Testament.

The New King James Version reads as follows: "Watch therefore, and pray always that you may be counted worthy to escape all these things that will come to pass, and to stand before the Son of Man."

ISIS: The Church's Wake-Up Call!

The Today's English Version says: "Be watchful and pray always that you will have strength to go safely through all these things that will happen, and to stand before the Son of Man" (Luke 2:36) (Emphasis mine).

Muslims teach that Judas was substituted for Jesus and that Judas was crucified in Jesus' stead on the cross. They further claim that Jesus will come to earth on the Last Day to convert Christians to Islam, and will kill those who refuse to submit or convert.

This teaching is in concert with their mistaken belief that Islam will conquer and rule the world forever! What a cruel lie! Christians, Jews, as well as, the Muslims, and others, are being and will be thrice deceived!

1. Paul wrote: "Let no man deceive you by any means; for that day (the Day of Christ's coming) and the Rapture (caught to meet him in the air day) shall not come, except there comes a falling away first, and that man of sin be revealed, the son of perdition" (2 Thessalonians 2:3). This is the Antichrist, the Muslim's Dajjal! He comes with false miracles and signs. "The coming of the lawless one is according to the

working of Satan, with all power, signs and lying wonders" (2 Thessalonians 2:9).

2. Again Paul wrote: "Now the Spirit speaketh expressly, that in the latter times some shall depart from the faith, giving heed to seducing spirits, and doctrines of demons; (such as happened to Muhammed in the cave and is happening with young people today.) Speaking lies in hypocrisy; having their conscience seared with a hot iron" (1 Timothy 4:1-3).

3. Once the Antichrist (the beast) and the false prophet are on the scene together in Revelation 13:1-8, drawing people into false worship and false allegiance by way of false teachings (Islam) and false wonders, we find Paul again saying: "And for this cause (unbelief)--God shall send them strong delusion that they should believe a lie; that they all might be damned who believe not the truth, the Gospel, but had pleasure in unrighteous" (2 Thessalonians 2:11-12).

Why Persecution and Martyrdom?

Persecution and martyrdom are a part of the mystery of the cross to which the church-- the body of Christ has been called. Paul wrote to the persecuted saints at Thessalonica saying, "Therefore we sent Timothy…to establish you…that no one should be shaken by these afflictions; for you…yourselves know that we are appointed to this" (I Thessalonians 3:1-3).

Paul stated in Romans 8:18, "I reckon that our present sufferings are not worthy to be compared with the glory that will be revealed in us."

In 2 Timothy 2:8-13 Paul expounds this mystery a bit further. Here he says: "Remember Jesus Christ, raised from the dead, descended from David. This is my gospel, for which I am suffering even to the point of being chained like a criminal. But God's Word is not chained.

"Therefore I endure everything for the sake of the elect; (God's chosen people) that they too may obtain the salvation (the glorified body) that is in Christ Jesus with eternal glory. Here is a trustworthy saying:

"If we died with him, we will also live with him, If we endure (suffer with him without fainting) we will also reign with him." (NIV Version)

Now to return to our book title, "ISIS – The Church's Wake Up Call." Let us call to remembrance the fact that Islam conquered much of the known world and ruled that portion for 1400 years! Let's read about the apparent antichrist described by John in Revelation 6:2: "I looked and there before me was a white horse! Its rider held a bow, and he was given a crown, and he rode out as a conqueror bent on conquest…Then another horse came, a fiery red one. Its rider was given power to take peace from the earth… To him was given a large sword (a slaughtering weapon)."

Why Persecution and Martyrdom?

Verse 9 says: "When he opened the fifth seal, I saw under the altar the souls (the blood) of those who had been slain (slaughtered) because of the word of God and the testimony they had maintained. These souls cried out to God; 'How long, Sovereign Lord, holy and true until you judge the inhabitants of the earth and avenge our blood'? Then each of them was given a white robe and they were told to wait a little longer (a little season) until the number of their fellow servants and brothers who were to be killed as they had been was completed" (Revelation 6:9-11).

Here we have the historical and the prophetic picture of Christian martyrs who were killed in the past (the first 300 years of church history) and those who are being martyred now, by ISIS, and other Muslims, and those who will be martyred right up to the final 3 ½ years of "Jacob's trouble" or "the great tribulation;" just before the great God and Savior returns and delivers His people (Christians and Jews) out of the hand of the enemy-the Antichrist (Titus 2:13). This is our "blessed hope!"

Revelation Chapter 7 references an uncountable multitude of transitioned saints of God, out of every nation, tribe and tongue (the church) standing before the throne. "These are they who have come out of the great tribulation, they have washed their robes and made them white in the blood of the Lamb." (Revelation 7:14)

It was the Roman Empire which persecuted Christians in the beginning (the first 300 years) of the church's existence. But since 610 A.D., the church's chief persecutor has been Islam! Their theme is death, while the church's theme is life! The Arabs of Arabia had 360 "gods" in their main place of worship before the "revelation" of Allah, the moon god, one of the 360 gods.

The prophet Daniel correctly describes the Muslim Antichrist in the following manner: "He shall regard neither the god of his fathers, nor the desire of women, nor regard any god; for he shall exalt himself above them all. But in their place he shall honor a god of fortresses (war): a god which his fathers did not know..." (Daniel 7:31-38; 2 Thessalonians 2:4)

These verses describe both Antiochus Epiphanes (a 2nd century B.C. Greek king who hated and severely

Why Persecution and Martyrdom?

persecuted the Jewish people) a type of the Antichrist, as well as the Antichrist himself. His god of fortresses is a god of war! So the Muslim's "god" is a god of war! Their religion is a religion of force and death!

Whereas it is the plan of Satan to visit suffering and affliction on the Christians and Jews; it is in God's will and purpose that all Christians, like Paul, should know Christ and the power of his resurrection, and the fellowship of his sufferings, being made conformable unto his death (Philippians 3:10).

Paul instructs us further in God's plan for His church to endure, redemptive suffering that leads to victory in Christ. Paul wrote: "As it is written; For thy sake we are killed all the day long; we are accounted as sheep for the slaughter; "Nay, in all these things we are more than conquerors through him that loved us" (Romans 8:36-37).

A Deeper Look into Islam's False Prophecies

Having studied many books on Islam over the past twenty years or so; I must say that I have gained a very good knowledge of the religion of Muhammed. It is reported that when Muhammed received his first and major "revelation" in a cave near Mecca, Arabia, that he heard a voice saying, "Allah is the only true god, and you, Muhammed are my messenger (or prophet)."

During that reported encounter, it is said that a spirit being squeezed Muhammed extremely tightly on three occasions, wherein it nearly squeezed his breath out of him, commanding him to "recite, recite." That is, to recite the creed that the spirit had spoken to him mentioned above. That creed today is called the Shahadatan. It is said that Muhammed was quite frightened and thought that he would die. So in his fearful state of mind, he climbed up a mountainside with the intention of jumping off and killing himself. However, again, it is reported that a spirit showed up and said, "I am Gabriel," and overshadowed him with peace. Whereupon, Muhammed climbed down from the mountain and ran to his favored wife (out of many wives) for comfort and assurance of his experience.

From Joel Richardson's recent book, THE ISLAMIC ANTICHRIST on page 73, we read the following statement: "The Dajjal is described as a deceiver who will have and who will temporarily hold power over the whole earth:

"The prophet was warning us that in the last days there would be someone who would deceive all of humanity. The Dajjal will possess power over this world. Thus, Muslims must be careful not to have the love of the world in their hearts so they won't leave their religion and follow him. He will be able to heal the sick by wiping his hands on them, like Jesus did, but with this deceit the Dajjal will lead people down the path to hell. Thus, the Dajjal is the false Messiah, or Antichrist. He will pretend to be the Messiah, and deceive people by showing them amazing powers. The Dajjal's name or title means (the Liar/Deceiver)." Doesn't he sound like the devil indeed? Jesus said, "He (the devil) is a liar and the father of it" (John 8:44).

Joel Richardson (2015) further recorded on page 74 of his book, that the Dajjal will be a false miracle worker. "The Dajjal will have powers of the devil. He will terrorize the Muslims into following him, converting them to unbelief. He will conceal the truth and bring forth falsehood." (This sounds very much like the lawless one of whom Paul wrote in 2 Thessalonians 2:9-10.)

Again Joel Richardson points out from Muslim tradition (eschatology): "The Jews await the false Jewish Messiah, while we wait with Allah's help… the Mahdi and Jesus, peace be upon him. "Jesus' pure hands will murder the false Jewish Messiah here in the City of Lod, in Palestine. Palestine will be, as it was in the past, a graveyard for the invaders" (2015, p. 76).

Can you see the kind of garbage Muslims are fed? And they believe it, hook, line and sinker! They actually believe that Jesus is one of them - that Allah spared

Jesus from dying on the cross, and that Jesus ascended to heaven alive, and will return to earth on the Last Day to do the bidding of Allah. What a lie!

Understanding God's Timeline as We Approach the End

We began this book declaring: "ISIS, THE CHURCH'S WAKE UP CALL!"

As surely as the Islamic attack on America's former Twin Towers on 9/11 was America's wake-up call, so too, ISIS is the Church's wake-up call!

People go about their daily business as though there is no God, no church, no gospel and no end to this world system. But according to the Bible, and events predicted therein –there is an end of this world system as recorded in God's Word.

The Apostle Paul wrote: "Then comes the end, when He (Christ) delivers the Kingdom to God the

Father, when He puts an end to all rule and all authority and power.

"For He must reign till He has put all enemies under His feet. The last enemy that will be destroyed is death." (I Corinthians 15:24-26)

Yes, the end of this world system is coming and sooner than most think!

What is God's timeline? Well, He has more than one, but we are interested in His 2,000 year cycles as recorded in the Bible, where He has a change of relationship with mankind at the end of each 2000 year cycle. In Abraham God found a man He could call friend and imputed His righteousness to him because of Abraham's faith. Jesus, God's Son, died on the cross, so that all men could receive God's righteousness by faith!

We understand from Bible history that Adam lived around 4,000 B.C. From Adam to Abraham are 2,000 years. That is, Abraham lived around 2,000 B.C. As we observe further, we will see that from Abraham to

Understanding God's Timeline as We Approach the End

Jesus Christ is another 2,000 years– equaling a total of 4,000 years!

Let us recall the prophetic words of the Apostle Peter: "But beloved, do not forget this one thing, that with the Lord one day is as a thousand years, and a thousand years as one day" (2 Peter 3:8).

Beloved, this is God's way of reckoning time! One day to Him equals one thousand years! Therefore, as we apply this method of reckoning time, we find that nearly six days (or six thousand years) have passed since God created Adam. From Jesus to present day, nearly two thousand years have passed! This totals nearly 6,000 years since Adam! Once one adds the millennium of 1,000 years, it brings us to 7,000 years, God's number of completion! It brings us to God's eternal Kingdom of joy and peace in the Presence of God (Psalm 16:11).

If we apply God's method of reckoning time, we will see that during the years, two of the 2,000 year periods are completed. And at the end of the third 2000 year period, some 6,000 years of human history will have been completed!

ISIS: The Church's Wake-Up Call!

What we can deduce from the Bible is that Christ will return to earth from heaven, as His Word promised (Acts 1:11); and because God is a God of exactness, precision and perfection, Jesus must return between 2030 A.D. and 2033 A.D.--depending on which biblical scholars' dates one chooses to follow.

Jesus was crucified in April (In Nisan the first month of the Jewish calendar) of 30 A.D. He died, was buried and arose on the third day, according to the Scriptures (I Corinthians 15:3-4). On the day that Christ died He fulfilled the historic Feast of the Lord known as Passover! At the exact moment when the priest sacrificed the Passover lamb, Christ was crucified on the cross, thus fulfilling the Feast of the Passover.

When Christ rose from the dead, having been buried for three days and three nights, he arose, thus fulfilling the Feast of Firstfruits (I Corinthians 15:23).

On a Sunday, fifty days after Resurrection Sunday, the Risen Christ fulfilled the Feast of Pentecost by pouring out His Spirit upon the 120 disciples assembled in the upper room (Acts 2:1-4, 33). Therefore, both the Feasts of Passover and Pentecost were fulfilled in 30 A.D.!

There remains one more Feast of the Lord to be fulfilled, yea, the Feast of Tabernacles, including the Feast of Trumpets, The Day of Atonement, and the Feast of the Ingathering or booths (Leviticus 23:23-33).

This last and final Feast, of the three major Feasts of the Lord, is celebrated on our Gregorian calendar in September-October. Just as the previous two major Feasts had their fulfillments in the Passover (death of Christ) and Pentecost, (the birth of the Church) so this last and final Feast of the Lord, shall mark the Second Coming of the Lord (I Thessalonians 3:13; 4:16-17)! He's coming for his saints and with His saints.

What am I really saying? According to the aforementioned biblical (God's) time table of events, our Lord Jesus should return at the point when 2,000 years have been fulfilled, since the cross, His resurrection, and the birthing of the church--30 A.D. to 33 A.D. 2,000 years after the events and dates mentioned above, places us at 2030 A.D. to 2033 A.D.!

No, I am not attempting to predict the day nor the hour wherein the Son of man cometh." (Matthew 24:36) However, according to the Apostle Paul, we can know "the times and seasons" of the Lord's coming. God has not left us ignorant of His "appointed times" nor Feasts (I Thessalonians 5:1)! No, we are not date setting! But we are calculating time as God does, on His time cycles of 2,000 year periods!

The Apostle Paul was an Israelite who was quite familiar with the three major "Feasts of the Lord" (There are seven Feasts in all). Yahweh commanded through Moses that these "Feasts" or "appointed times" be kept and observed by the Israelites throughout their generations. During the time Christ was on earth, the Jews had kept the "Feasts of the Lord," annually, for fourteen hundred years!

Paul wrote in I Thessalonians 5:1 the following: "But concerning the times and seasons, brethren, you have no need that I should write to you: ...But you, brethren, are not in darkness, so that this Day should overtake you as a thief." These Hebrew/Christian brethren knew these "Feasts" or "appointed times," or "set times" of the Lord, only too well!

Understanding God's Timeline as We Approach the End

English translators have rendered the Hebrew word moed as "seasons" and "feasts." This word is more accurately translated as "divine appointments"--times that God had determined beforehand to meet with his covenant people, and to intervene in human history. He will do that in the Rapture of the church at the Second Coming of the Lord.

Let's listen to the words of this God of order, precision and predetermination: "And the Lord spoke to Moses, saying, speak to the children of Israel, and say to them: 'the feasts of the Lord, which you shall proclaim to be Holy convocations (or dress rehearsals), these are My Feasts" (Leviticus 23:2-3).

Therefore, these long standing "divine appointments" (feasts or convocations) have been God's dress rehearsals for the fulfillment of the following foreordained events: The Cross of Calvary, the Resurrection and the Ascension of our Lord Christ, and the outpouring of the Holy Spirit, by which Christ birthed His church. And now, some 2,000 years later, Christ will return and receive His Bride, the Church, in the midair, and glorify her there (Colossians 3:4; Romans 8:17). He will fulfill the last and final feast we call "The Feast of Tabernacles in His return to earth. Christ will descend to earth and also fulfill the words of Jude: "Behold the Lord comes with ten thousands of His saints, to execute judgement on all among them of all their ungodly deeds which they have committed in an ungodly way" (Jude 1:14-15) (NIV Version).

When Christ returns and fulfills the Feast of Tabernacles He will fulfill the Feast of Trumpets as recorded in I Thessalonians 4:16; Matthew 24:31 and other related verses. Christ will also fulfill the Feast of the Ingathering or Feast of Booths as recorded in Matthew 24:31 and in Ephesians 1:10 and 2 Thessalonians 2:1.

Ephesians 1:10 says: "That in the dispensation of the fullness of times he might gather together in one all things in Christ, both which are in heaven and on earth, even in him."

2 Thessalonians 2:1 says: "Now we beseech you brethren by the coming of our Lord Jesus Christ, and by our gathering together unto him…"

ISIS, The Church's Wake-Up Call!

Let us return to the title of this book:

'ISIS, The Church's Wake Up Call!' Just as we have shown you in the previous chapter that God has a specific time--for fulfilling His prophecies and purposes, so too, God has other less precise signs to help us locate where we are in His prophetic scheme of things.

We have shown you from the book of Daniel (Chapter 7) that Islam is the fourth beast that Daniel identifies in this chapter. The "little horn" out of this fourth beast, Islam, is none other than the Antichrist or his precursor, Antiochus Epiphanes. This Greek king was of the Seleucid Empire, who reigned from 175 B.C. to 164 B.C. He was a vicious enemy of the Jews and desecrated their temple with swine's flesh and persecuted them severely.

Apostle John in Revelation 13:2 recorded that he saw a beast like a leopard, his feet were like the feet of a bear, and his mouth like the mouth of a lion." The beast that John saw is a composite of the "beasts" which Daniel described in his vision recorded in Daniel 7:3-7. The beasts represented "four kingdoms"(or empires) which were: Babylon, Medo Persia, Greco-Roman and Islam. Daniel stated further, "And there in this (little) horn, were eyes like the eyes of a man, and a mouth speaking pompous words" (Daniel 7:8).

John the Revelator picks up Daniel's vision and carries it forward. John wrote: "The dragon (the devil) gave him (the Antichrist) his power, his throne, and his great authority." Again beloveds, this "beast" or kingdom is none other than Islam! John continues: "And I saw one of his heads (one of the seven heads) as if it had been mortally wounded, and his deadly wound was healed. And all the world marveled and followed the beast" (Revelation 13:3).

ISIS, The Church's Wake-Up Call!

Once again, the deadly wound to the head of the beast (Islam) is nothing more than the Islamic Caliphate (Ruling Head) that was defeated and dethroned in Istanbul, Turkey, in 1924! This was the Ottoman Empire. This Caliphate was brought down by Christian nations--Britain, France, Poland, etc. The Muslims were a world power for 1400 years.

The prophet Daniel described the fourth "beast" in this wise: "After this I saw in the night visions, and behold, a fourth beast, dreadful and terrible, exceedingly strong it had huge iron teeth, it was devouring, breaking in pieces, and trampling the residue (the other three kingdoms or empires) with its feet. It was different from all the beasts that there were before it" (Daniel 7:7). It was religious, political and militant.

I am not alone in believing that the fourth beast of Daniel was Arab Muslim! Some names of note in history and in the church subscribed to this view. A few such noted persons are: Sophronius, Patriarch of Jerusalem, (560-635 A.D.), John of Damascus, (676-749 A.D.), John Wesley, Martin Luther, John Calvin, (1509-1564 A.D.), Johnathan Edwards, (1703-1758 A.D.), Bishop Fulton J. Sheen, (1950's), Walid Shoebat, a contemporary Christian Prophecy scholar, and Joel Richardson, also a contemporary Christian, filmmaker, New York Times best seller of several prophetic books, and an expert on the Middle East and Islam. I consider that I am in very good, distinguished company!

As I have fore stated, the Islamic Caliphate was located in different countries over Islam's 1400 years of rule. Some of these countries were Egypt, Iraq, Sudan and others. The last and probably the most important of these countries is Turkey, where the Ottoman Empire ruled for many years and met its demise in 1924. All Caliphs are supposed to be descendants of Muhammed and Shiites.

Turkey is located due north of Jerusalem and is an Islamic nation. Ezekiel prophesied that God would bring Gog (whom some scholars believe to be the Antichrist) "up from the far north and bring you against the mountains of Israel. You shall fall upon the mountain of Israel ...You and all your troops and the peoples who are with you. I will give to the birds of prey of every sort and to the beasts of the field to be devoured" (Ezekiel 39:1-4).

Turkey is an Islamic nation as are all the other nations in the Gog/Magog coalition (See Ezekiel, 38:3-6). Please note that Russia, a non-Muslim nation, is not named among the members of this ungodly coalition.

Magog encompasses Asia Minor, an area identified by Josephus as, "the land of the Scythians" (Colossians 3:11). Ancient Scythia includes regions of Asia Minor (Turkey) and several Central Asian states… These are all Muslim nations (Shoebat, 2008, pp. 254-255).

The Time Has Arrived for a Revived Muslim Caliphate

For the past ninety plus years the Muslim Caliphate has been wounded with "a deadly wound." Muslims have been out of power and playing "second fiddle" to Western powers. Muslims have been stirring since the late 1970's and the 1980's. They sensed the weakness of America during Jimmy Carter's Presidency (1977-1981). They saw their chance to begin rising up ("being resurrected") again.

The Ayatollah Khomeini who had been exiled to Paris, returned to Iran to regain power. He reinstated Fundamentalist Islam into Iran at that time. Iran had been a democracy of sorts. The Shah of Iran fled to the U.S. and died there. There was an uprising wherein Fundamentalist Iranians took over the U.S. Embassy

ISIS: The Church's Wake-Up Call!

for nearly a year. Ronald Reagan became the U.S. President in 1981. America got our Foreign Service people out of Iran, and Russia chose to invade Afghanistan, an Islamic nation.

The Afghan fighters, the Mujahadeen, under the leadership of Osama Bin Laden, defeated the Russians badly and drove them out in disgrace. Again, these developments emboldened the Muslims even more.

Let us take note that Muslims know their history. They are very aware that they ruled much of the world for 1400 years! Saddam Hussein knew Iraq's history when he attacked Kuwait. He knew that Iraq had previously owned Kuwait until the British re-drew the geographical lines there.

Likewise, Osama Bin Laden was well aware of Islam's history and former world leadership. He was plugged into Islam's longing to be on top again, when he orchestrated the destruction of the "Great Satan's" (America's) Twin Towers!

ISIS and other Jihadist Muslim groups have begun their rise to restore their international Caliphate.

The Time Has Arrived for a Revived Muslim Caliphate

According to Bible Scriptures we have cited in Daniel 7 and Revelation 13, Islam's "deadly wound" will be healed. Their Caliphate, will have world rulership for a time. It will be restored by God's permission (Daniel 7:23-25; Revelation. 13:1-10). But in the end the saints (Old and New Testament saints) win! (Daniel 7:21-22, 26-27)

Finally, in light of the current threats of and attacks of ISIS on Christians and Jews, the book of Daniel, says "At that time Michael shall stand up, the great prince who stands watch over the sons of your people, and there shall be a time of trouble, (tribulation) such as never was since there was a nation, even to that time (Matthew 24:21). And at that time your people shall be delivered, everyone who is found written in the book" (Daniel 12:1).

As we approach the conclusion of this book, "ISIS THE CHURCH'S WAKE UP CALL"; let us review some Bible passages that call on the Church to awaken! Jesus taught in the parable of virgins, "But while the bridegroom was delayed, they all (the virgins or the church) slumbered and slept. And at midnight a cry was heard: 'Behold, the bridegroom is coming; go out to meet him" (Matthew 25:5-6)!

The Apostle Paul picks up on this idea of the need for the church to awaken out of its sleep when he says, "Awake, you who sleep, Arise from the dead, and Christ will give you light (revelation and understanding)" (Ephesians 5:14).

Again the Apostle Paul challenges the church on its need to keep awake! He writes, "For you yourselves know perfectly that the day of the Lord so comes as a thief in the night...But you brethren are not in darkness, so that this Day should overtake you as a thief...Therefore let us not sleep, as others do, but let us watch and be sober. But let us who are of the day be sober (serious), putting on the breast plate of faith and love (not of hate and death, as the Muslims do), and as a helmet the hope of salvation (I Thessalonians 5:2-8).

Final Chapter

We must include one more passage of Scripture from the Apostle Paul regarding the slumbering church and its need to awake from its sleeping condition! For truly the church is largely asleep with regard to biblical prophecy, and the nearness of the Lord's return and the Rapture.

Today, the church is caught up in more worldliness than godliness. It appears to be more involved in relating to the world in the areas of entertainment; mega productions; mega churches trying to outdo other mega churches; fashions and materialism; than in being aware of the Lord's coming!

Jesus warned Christian believers of our day in His parable of the Sower: "Still others, like seed sown among thorns, hear the word; but the cares of this life, the deceitfulness of riches and the desires for other things come in and choke the word, making it unfruitful" (Mark 4:18-19).

Paul wrote "And do this, understanding the present time. The hour has come for you to wake up from your slumber, because our salvation (the coming of the Lord) is nearer than when we first believed. The night is nearly over; the day is almost here. So let us put aside the deeds of darkness, and put on the armor of light" (Romans 13:11-12 NIV).

We cannot conclude this book on a negative note, but rather on a redemptive one. The Lord has promised the church a great awakening—a great miracle, global revival before Jesus Christ returns to receive His church unto Himself. Through the prophet Isaiah the Lord speaks to His church:

> "Arise, shine;
> For your light has come!
> And the glory of the Lord is risen upon you.
> For behold, the darkness shall cover the earth
> And deep darkness the people;

Final Chapter

But the Lord will arise over you,
And His glory will be seen upon you…"
(Isaiah 60:1-2)

This will be a mighty move of the Lord in and upon His people, the church, in awesome signs, wonders and miracles—that will sweep millions of souls into God's Kingdom.

Amos the prophet spoke of the coming end-time Great Awakening and great revival on this wise: "Behold the days are coming," says the Lord, "When the plowman shall overtake the reaper, And the treader of grapes him who sows seed" (Amos 9:13).

Again the prophet Isaiah speaks to the Church and says:

"Awake, awake!
Put on your strength, O Zion…
"How beautiful upon the mountains
Are the feet of him who brings good news,
"Who proclaims peace,
Who brings glad tidings of good things,
Who proclaims salvation" (Isaiah 52:1, 7)

ISIS: The Church's Wake-Up Call!

While ISIS and other Islamic hordes are slaughtering Christians and Jews in this end time, God is going to move to save souls by the thousands! The Church is going to be empowered by the Holy Spirit once again, as in the early days of the Church. Once again, as said in Foxe's Book of the Martyrs, "The blood of the martyrs is the seed of the Church." The more the enemies of Christ kill Christians, the more the Church will grow, until it reaches a number "which no man could number. These are the ones who come out of the great tribulation, and washed their robes and made them white in the blood of the Lamb" (Revelation 7:9, 14).

Finally, we close with John the Revelator's words: "Now I saw heaven opened, and behold, a white horse. And He who sat on him, was called Faithful and True, and in righteousness, He judges and makes war... And the armies in heaven--(the church triumphant, or the dead in Christ) clothed in fine linen, white and clean, followed Him on white horses" (Revelation 19:11, 14).

Let us inject some companion verses from Isaiah the prophet on Christ's return to earth in wrath, to repay his enemies, the Muslims, who had put a hurting on His Church and the Jews, the natural seed of Abraham.

Isaiah wrote: "Who is this who comes from Edom, (Saudi Arabia, et al.) with crimson-stained garments from Bozrah (in Edom)? This One Who is glorious in His apparel, striding triumphantly in the greatness of His might? 'It is I, (the One) Who speaks in righteousness (proclaiming vindication), mighty to save!' 'Why is your apparel splashed with red, and, Your garments like one who treads in the winepress?' 'I have trodden the winepress alone… I trod them in My anger and trampled them in My wrath; and their life blood is sprinkled upon My garments, and I stained all My raiment.' For the day of vengeance is in My heart and My year of redemption (the year of My redeemed) has come'" (Isaiah 63:1-4) (Amplified Bible).

"Now out of His mouth goes a sharp sword, that with it He should strike the nations (Islamic nations in particular). And He Himself will rule them with a rod of iron. He Himself treads the winepress of the fierceness and wrath of Almighty God. And He has on His robe and on His thigh a name written:

"KING OF KINGS AND LORD OF LORDS," (Revelation 19:11, 14-16)
And I say with John,
"Even So Come, Lord Jesus!" (Revelation 22:20b)

Bibliography

(2014) "Islam religion of peace or war." The Truth. Retrieved from http://www.c4israel.us/c4i-us/download/common/islam-religion-of-peace-or-war.pdf. Also distributed by the 700 Club.

THE HOLY BIBLE: King James, New King James, New International Version and the Amplified Bible versions.

Foxe, J., & Forbush, W. B. (1978). Foxe's Book of Martyrs. Grand Rapids, Mich: Baker.

Rafiabadi, H. N. (2009). The Quran illustrated (Surah-al-fatiha). New Delhi: Sarup Book Publishers.

Richardson, J. (2015). The Islamic Antichrist: The shocking truth about the real nature of the beast.

Safa, R. F. (1996). Inside Islam: Exposing and reaching the world of Islam. Orlando, FL: Creation House.
Shoebat, W., & Richardson, J. (2008). God's war on terror: Islam, prophecy and the Bible. United States: Top Executive Media.

About the Author

Dr. Aaron B. Claxton has been in Christ for nearly 60 years and has preached the Gospel for nearly 60 years.

Dr. Claxton is the father of seven children, which initially and graciously began with his precious firstborn daughter, Gayle.

He has been married to his lovely wife, Deborah, for nearly 50 years. They are the proud parents of six children (four boys and two girls), all have been called into the five-fold ministry. The Claxtons are also blessed with a host of grandchildren and great grandchildren.

Dr. Claxton's academic background includes earned degrees from Morgan State University, from the Mount Royal College of the Bible and from St. Mary's Seminary and University, where he pursued the academics for the Doctor of Ministry degree. He completed that degree in 1996 at the Family Bible Seminary. Dr. Claxton has been awarded two honorary Doctorate degrees from Christian International University. They are the Doctor of Divinity and the Doctor of Laws degrees. He received his PhD degree in Biblical Studies from Family Bible Seminary in May 2003.

In addition to this prolific masterpiece, Dr. Claxton has authored over thirty (30) books of which nine (9) are published:

1 - *"God's Plan for the Sons of Ham – a future and a hope"*
2 - *"The Biblical View of the Rapture and the Second Coming"*
3 - *"Farrakhan, Islam and Jesus the Messiah"*
4 - *"The Blessing of the Lord is Upon the Tither"*
5 - *"First Fruits the Missing Offering"*
6 - *"Possessing Our Earthly Inheritance Now!"*
7 - *"Caught Up to Meet Him"*
8 - *"Understanding the Root, the Causes and the Remedy of the Middle East Conflict"*

Apostle Claxton, along with his wife, Deborah, founded and pastored the New Creation Christian Church in Baltimore, Maryland for twenty-three years. He has taught at three Bible Colleges and is well traveled, having preached the Gospel across America and in sixteen nations around the world.

Dr. Claxton stands in the offices of Apostle and Bishop, formally overseeing one hundred plus churches in the U.S., and in East and West Africa and is presently being established in a global, apostolic ministry, along with his wife, Deborah in her apostolic ministry. His oldest son, Apostle Aaron Bryan Claxton, along with his wife, Sheila, now pastor the headquarters church in Baltimore, which Dr. Claxton founded in 1968.

www.ingramcontent.com/pod-product-compliance
Lightning Source LLC
Chambersburg PA
CBHW070550300426
44113CB00011B/1851